HOW ⚙ THINGS ⊚ WORK

CARS
BIKES
TRAINS

AND OTHER
LAND
MACHINES

IAN GRAHAM

Kingfisher Books

NEW YORK

KINGFISHER BOOKS
Grisewood & Dempsey Inc.
95 Madison Avenue
New York, New York 10016

First American edition 1993
2 4 6 8 10 9 7 5 3 1

Library of Congress Cataloging-in-Publication Data
Graham, Ian, 1953–
[How land machines work]
Cars, bikes, trains, and other land machines / Ian Graham. — 1st
American ed.
p. cm. — (How things work)
Published in Great Britain under title: How land machines work.
Summary: Text, illustrations, and diagrams introduce the parts,
operation, and uses of cars, motorcycles, trucks, and other land
vehicles.
1. Vehicles — Juvenile literature. 2. Railroads — Juvenile
literature. [1. Vehicles.] I. Title. II. Series: How things work
(New York, N.Y.)
TL147.G67 1993
629.04'9 — dc20 92-33587 CIP AC

ISBN 1-85697-872-9 (lib. bdg.)
ISBN 1-85697-871-0 (pbk.)

Printed in Hong Kong

Series editor: Jackie Gaff
Series designer: David West Children's Books
Author: Ian Graham
Cover illustration: Micheal Fisher (Garden Studio)
Illustrators: Darren Fletcher pp. 38-9; Chris Forsey pp. 6-7,
20-1, 28-9, 34-5; Maltings Partnership pp. 12-13, 26-7;
Simon Tegg pp. 8-9, 16-17, 24-5, 30-1, 36-7; Ian Thompson
pp. 2-5, 14-15, 22-3; Ross Watton (Garden Studio)
pp. 10-11, 18-19, 32-3.
Research: A.R. Blann

The publishers would like to thank: David Jefferis;
AEG Westinghouse Transportation Systems, Inc.; BMW (GB)
Ltd; British Rail; Deutsche Bundesbahn; GEC Alsthom
Transportation Projects Ltd; Goodyear Great Britain Ltd;
Greater Manchester Passenger Transport Authority and
Executive; Honda; Iveco Ford Truck Ltd; Mitsubishi Motors;
Network SouthEast; Portman Lamborghini; Slam City Skates
(Russell Waterman); SNCF French Railways Ltd; Transrapid
International; Volkswagen Press; Volvo (GB) Ltd.

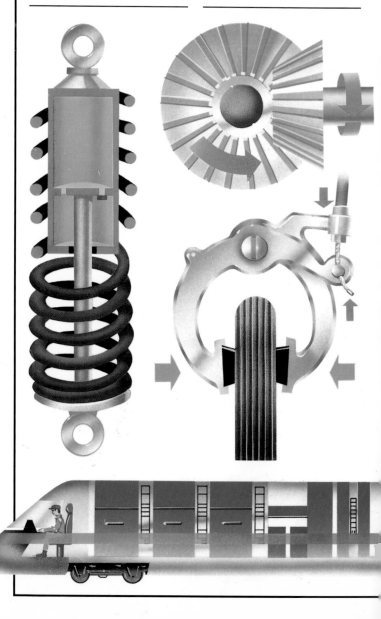

CONTENTS

FAMOUS FIRSTS ON LAND

In about 1493, the great Italian artist and inventor Leonardo da Vinci came up with the first design for a bicycle with pedals (it was probably never built, though).

In 1760, the first roller skates were made, by Joseph Merlin of Belgium.

△ In 1769, Frenchman Nicolas-Joseph Cugnot built the first land vehicle to move under its own power, a steam-powered military tractor.

△ In 1804, the English engineer Richard Trevithick built the first steam locomotive used to pull cars on rails.

▽ In 1825, the world's first public steam railroad opened, the Stockton and Darlington line, in England.

△ In about 1839, the first pedal-powered bicycle was built, by Scotsman Kirkpatrick Macmillan.

△ In 1863, the first four-wheel roller skates (fore-runners of modern skates) were made by American James Plimpton.

△ In 1869, in France, Pierre and Ernest Michaux built the first successful motorcycle. It had a steam engine.

△ In 1870, Englishman James Starley built the first high-wheeler bicycle.

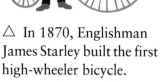

▽ In 1879, the first successful electric railroad was built, at the Berlin Trades Exhibition in Germany.

▽ In 1885, in Germany, Karl Benz built the first gasoline-engine car.

▽ In the same year, also in Germany, Gottlieb Daimler built the first motorcycle powered by a gasoline engine.

In 1888 the pneumatic tire was invented by Scotsman John Boyd Dunlop.

In 1916 the first mechanical windshield wipers appeared, in the U.S.

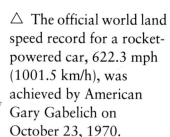

△ The official world land speed record for a rocket-powered car, 622.3 mph (1001.5 km/h), was achieved by American Gary Gabelich on October 23, 1970.

▽ The world's fastest car is *Thrust 2*, a jet-powered car driven by Briton Richard Noble to a speed of 633.5 mph (1019.5 km/h) on October 4, 1983.

The world's fastest train is the French TGV. It has reached the record speed of 320 mph (515 km/h).

▽ The world's fastest passenger-carrying maglev is the Japanese experimental MLU-001. In 1987, it reached 248 mph (400 km/h) on its specially built test track.

INTRODUCTION

The wheel was invented about 5,500 years ago, in what is now Iraq. Until then, people moved heavy loads by putting tree trunks under them to act as rollers.

The first wheels were just solid slices of tree linked by wooden axles. In areas where there weren't enough trees, or when tree trunks weren't big enough, wheels were made by joining wooden planks.

Then, about 4,000 years ago, the spoked wheel was invented. Spokes are slim struts between the rim and the hub of the wheel. This open construction was lighter than the solid wheel, but just as strong.

Spoke

Throughout history, people have looked for ways of traveling farther and faster. For thousands of years, the only way to do this was to ride on the back of a strong swift-moving animal, such as a horse or a camel. Then the invention of the wheel led to the first vehicles — animal-powered carts and carriages.

A long time later people figured out how to build engines to work machines, and a few intrepid inventors set about making a machine that could move under its own power. When these machines were first built, over 200 years ago, they were not very promising. Powered by dirty and noisy steam engines, they were slow and they often broke down.

The discovery of large underground oil fields in the 1860s finally gave engineers a plentiful supply of a really useful fuel. This rapidly led to the development of more powerful and reliable engines, and at last in the 1880s, to the first practical automobiles and motorcycles.

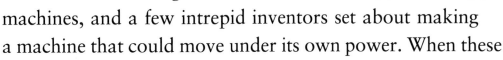

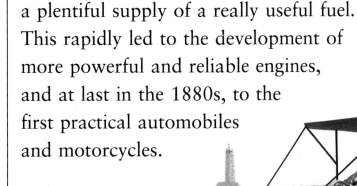

FOCUS ON FRICTION

Friction is a force that tries to stop things from moving, and which slows things down once they are moving. It's caused by two surfaces rubbing against each other.

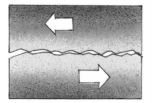

Roughness creates friction

All surfaces are rough. Even the smoothest block of metal looks jagged when seen under a microscope. When two surfaces try to slide past each other, their roughness makes them catch. This is friction.

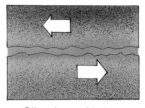

Oil reduces friction

One way to reduce friction is to keep the two surfaces apart. Materials called lubricants do this. Most are oily liquids that cling to surfaces and let them slip over each other smoothly.

ROLLING ALONG

Nearly every vehicle that travels on land has wheels to help it move. This is because as wheels roll along they reduce the effect of a slowing force called friction, which acts between them and the ground.

So wheels make movement easier. Just imagine how hard it would be to make a wheel-less skateboard move! In fact, if it wasn't for wheels, muscle-powered transporters such as skateboards and bicycles would be unusable, while cars and other powered vehicles would need gigantic engines.

☐ STEERING

A skateboard rider steers by leaning to one side or the other. The rider's weight makes the steering truck beneath the board tilt. This, in turn, makes the wheels swivel to the left or the right.

Truck

TEST IT OUT!

Here's a way to prove that wheels reduce friction. Tape a toy car's wheels down to stop them turning.

Put the car on a tray and stand a box next to it. Tilt the tray until the car starts to slide. Mark the tray's height on the box.

Now take the tape off the wheels. Tilt the tray again to see how much sooner and more quickly the car moves.

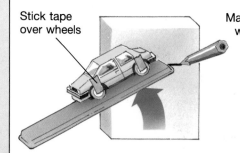

Stick tape over wheels

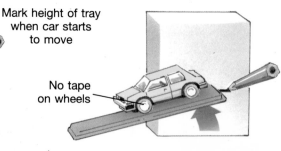

Mark height of tray when car starts to move

No tape on wheels

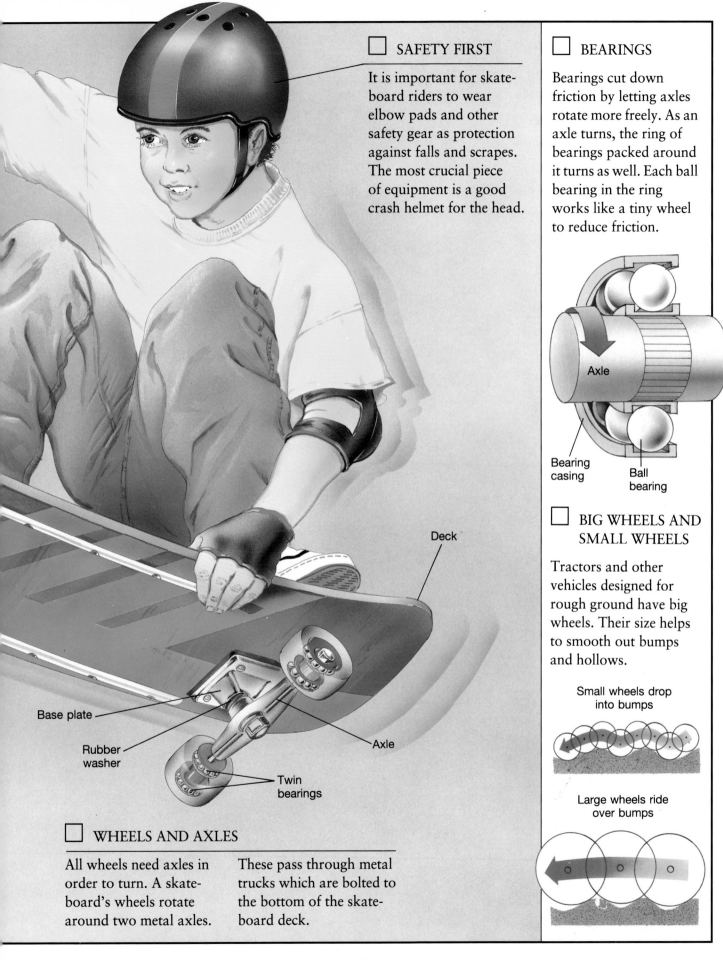

□ SAFETY FIRST

It is important for skateboard riders to wear elbow pads and other safety gear as protection against falls and scrapes. The most crucial piece of equipment is a good crash helmet for the head.

Deck

□ BEARINGS

Bearings cut down friction by letting axles rotate more freely. As an axle turns, the ring of bearings packed around it turns as well. Each ball bearing in the ring works like a tiny wheel to reduce friction.

Axle

Bearing casing

Ball bearing

□ BIG WHEELS AND SMALL WHEELS

Tractors and other vehicles designed for rough ground have big wheels. Their size helps to smooth out bumps and hollows.

Small wheels drop into bumps

Large wheels ride over bumps

Base plate

Rubber washer

Axle

Twin bearings

□ WHEELS AND AXLES

All wheels need axles in order to turn. A skateboard's wheels rotate around two metal axles.

These pass through metal trucks which are bolted to the bottom of the skateboard deck.

GETTING A GRIP

Land vehicles all use wheels, bearings, and lubricants to reduce friction. But friction is not always a bad thing. In some places, a little friction is essential.

For a vehicle to be able to move at all, its wheels have to grip and push against the ground. This grip is provided by friction. Without it, wheels would just spin around helplessly and the vehicle wouldn't move. Tires are designed to use friction to increase grip, and that's why wheels are fitted with them.

Tires are not just made of rubber, for rubber alone is not very strong. Instead, layers (called plies) of tough fabric are built up on a soft rubber liner, then covered by rubber tread and sidewalls. Two steel hoops called beads hold the tire in place on the wheel rim.

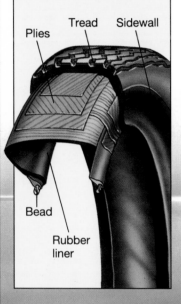

Plies
Tread   Sidewall
Bead
Rubber
liner

1 RACING TIRES

To go fast, racing bikes need tires that give good grip. In dry weather, smooth tires called slicks are used because they put the biggest area of rubber on the track.

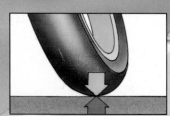

2 SLIPPING AND SLIDING

Slicks aren't suitable in the wet. They trap and ride on a film of water, losing their grip. This is called aquaplaning, and it makes vehicles skid.

☐ TOUGH TIRES

Off-road tire (rubber knobs)

Snow tire (metal studs)

Ice tire (metal spikes)

☐ VALVES

As air is pumped into a tire, the pressure (or push) of the air opens a valve. When the pump is taken away, the valve is held closed by the pressure of the air inside the tire.

Valve

Air pressure keeps valve closed

TEST IT OUT!

You can see the effect of aquaplaning in this easy experiment with a wooden block and a tray. Slide the block along the tray and watch how friction slows it down.

Now pour some water on the tray. The block will slide more easily, as it aquaplanes on the film of water.

Wooden block aquaplanes

3 WET WEATHER

Wet weather tires have grooved treads to let water escape from under them — it channels away along the grooves. The treads let the tire stay in contact with the track, providing grip.

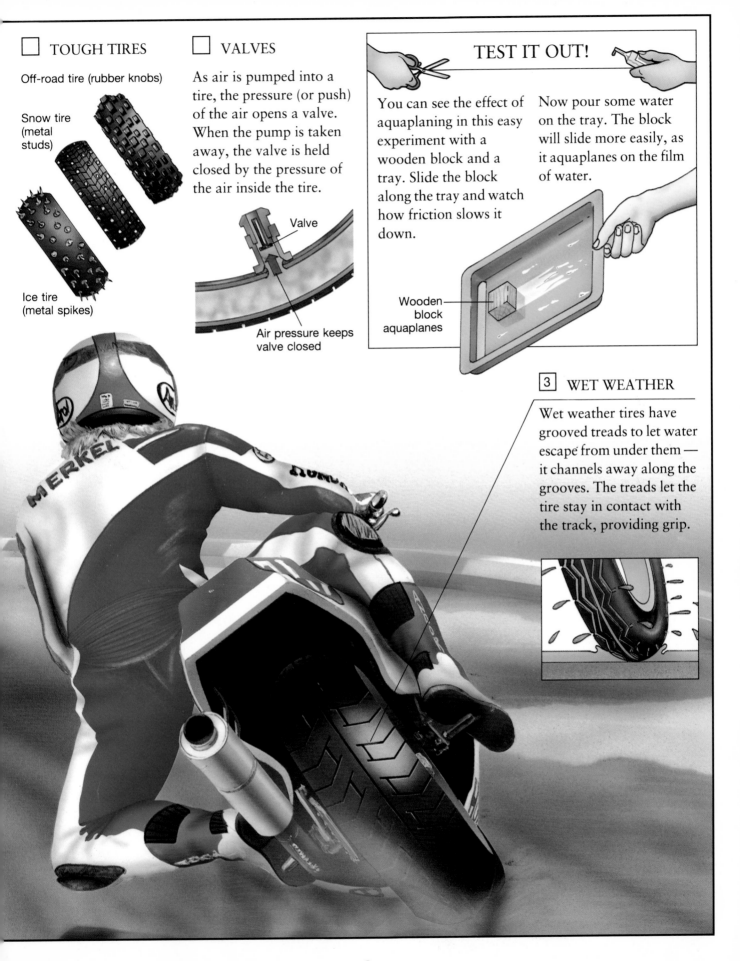

The famous British scientist Sir Isaac Newton discovered three laws of motion.

His first law states that an object won't move until acted on by a force, and that an object moving in a straight line will keep on doing so unless acted on by a force.

Isaac Newton (1642-1727)

A free-wheeling bicycle obeys this law. The bicycle doesn't keep moving forever, because friction from the ground and from the air (called air resistance or drag) slows it down.

Applying the brakes gives extra friction for a fast stop.

Air friction and ground friction act against the bicycle, slowing it down

PUTTING ON THE BRAKES

Because friction slows moving objects, it can be used to make vehicles brake and stop. Bicycle brakes work by pressing pads of tough material directly onto the wheel rims. Friction between the pads and the rims slows the wheel and brings the bicycle to a halt.

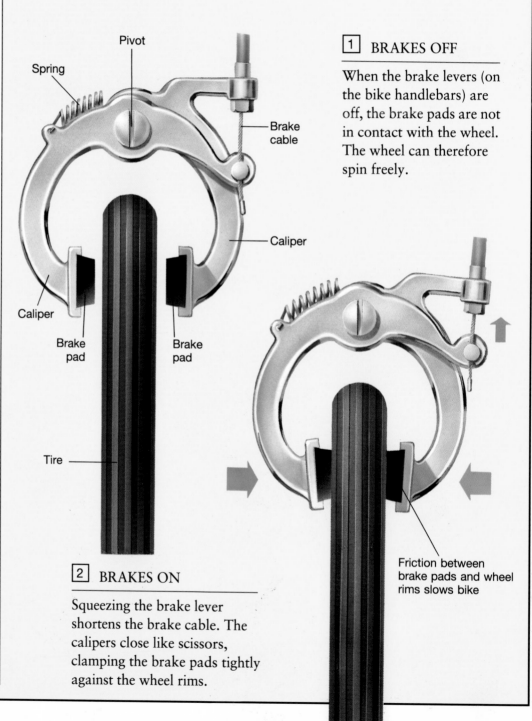

Spring

Pivot

Brake cable

Caliper

Caliper

Brake pad

Brake pad

Tire

Friction between brake pads and wheel rims slows bike

1 BRAKES OFF

When the brake levers (on the bike handlebars) are off, the brake pads are not in contact with the wheel. The wheel can therefore spin freely.

2 BRAKES ON

Squeezing the brake lever shortens the brake cable. The calipers close like scissors, clamping the brake pads tightly against the wheel rims.

DRUM AND DISC BRAKES

FOCUS ON SKIDDING

A car will skid if the driver presses the brake pedal so hard that the wheels lock (stop turning) before the car comes to a halt.

Anti-lock Braking Systems (ABS) prevent skidding by sensing when wheels are about to lock. They release and reapply the brakes up to 25 times a second. The car slows down instead of skidding out of control.

Most cars and trucks, and some motorcycles, are fitted with two types of brake. Disc brakes are usually fitted to the front wheels, and drum brakes to the rear. Some vehicles have disc brakes on all wheels. The different sorts of brake are named for the part of the wheel that the brake pads press against.

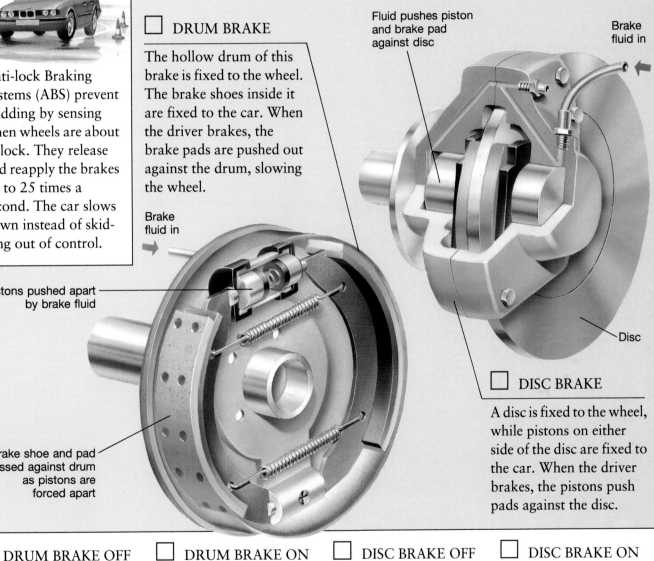

☐ DRUM BRAKE

The hollow drum of this brake is fixed to the wheel. The brake shoes inside it are fixed to the car. When the driver brakes, the brake pads are pushed out against the drum, slowing the wheel.

Brake fluid in

Fluid pushes piston and brake pad against disc

Brake fluid in

Pistons pushed apart by brake fluid

Brake shoe and pad pressed against drum as pistons are forced apart

Disc

☐ DISC BRAKE

A disc is fixed to the wheel, while pistons on either side of the disc are fixed to the car. When the driver brakes, the pistons push pads against the disc.

☐ DRUM BRAKE OFF

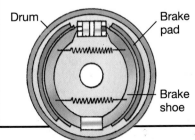

Drum

Brake pad

Brake shoe

☐ DRUM BRAKE ON

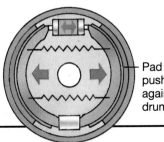

Pad pushes against drum

☐ DISC BRAKE OFF

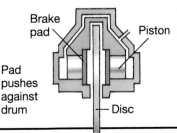

Brake pad

Piston

Disc

☐ DISC BRAKE ON

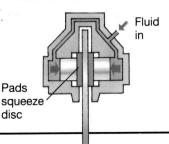

Fluid in

Pads squeeze disc

VEHICLE SYSTEMS

Manufacturers are now designing cars that cause less harm to the environment. For example, in some cars a device called a catalytic converter is fitted to the exhaust system, to "clean" up some harmful gases produced by the engine.

Catalytic converter cuts nitrogen oxide gases by 40%

Exhaust gases from engine

Car makers are looking for ways of re-using metal and plastic parts instead of throwing them away when a car is scrapped. This saves materials and reduces the problem of waste disposal.

Brakes are just one of the many systems that make up a modern vehicle. Each system does a different job. In the same way that human bodies have ways of taking in food and air, keeping cool, and getting rid of waste, vehicles have systems for taking in fuel, cooling the engine, and removing waste gases.

Different vehicles may have systems that do the same job, but in different ways. Bicycle brakes are operated by cable, for example, while car brakes are operated by oil pressure, and truck and train brakes by air pressure.

☐ RACING CAR

The systems of a Formula One car are designed to allow it to travel at high speed. Its odd-looking suspension holds the car low between the wheels instead of above them. Disc brakes on all wheels allow it to stop quickly if it has to.

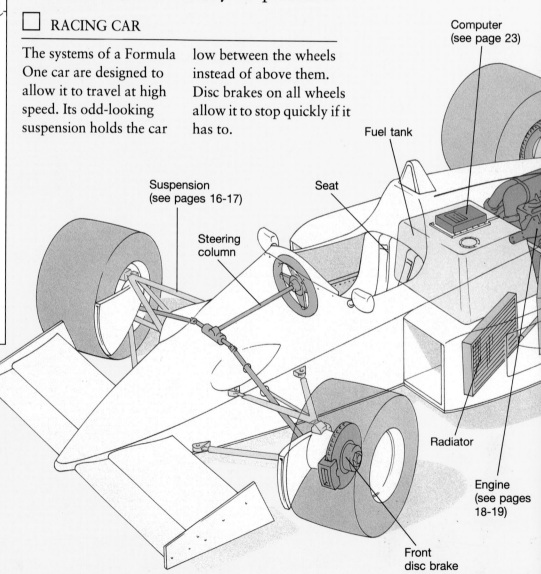

Computer
(see page 23)

Fuel tank

Suspension
(see pages 16-17)

Seat

Steering
column

Radiator

Engine
(see pages
18-19)

Front
disc brake

SYSTEMS KEY

- BRAKES
- ENGINE
- GEARS
- FUEL
- COMPUTER
- COOLING
- STEERING
- SUSPENSION
- EXHAUST

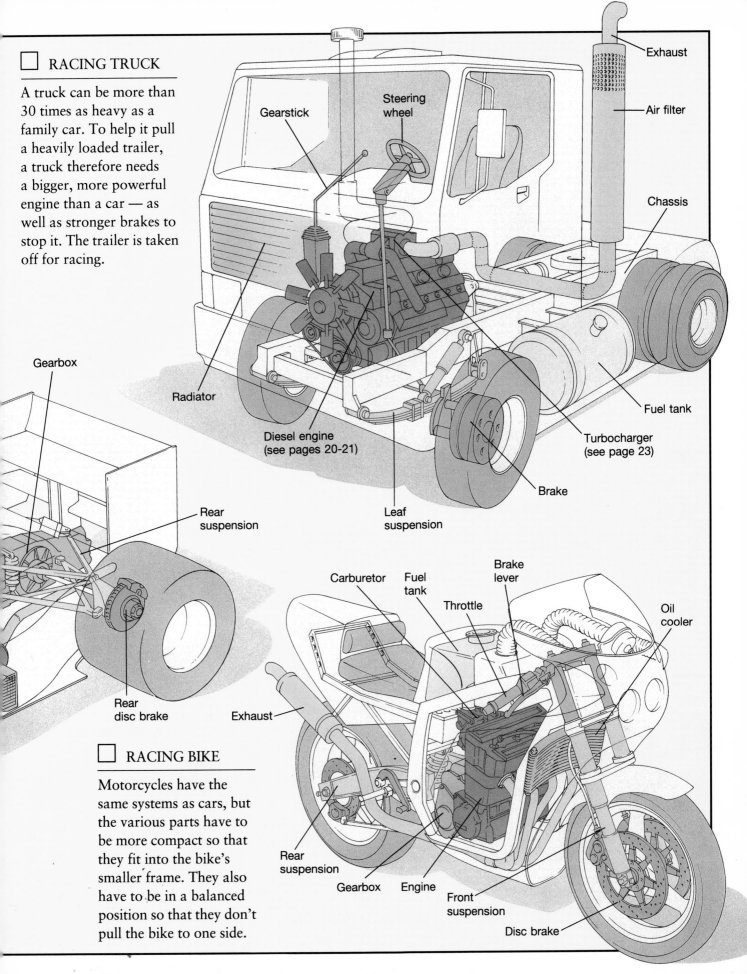

☐ RACING TRUCK

A truck can be more than 30 times as heavy as a family car. To help it pull a heavily loaded trailer, a truck therefore needs a bigger, more powerful engine than a car — as well as stronger brakes to stop it. The trailer is taken off for racing.

Exhaust

Air filter

Steering wheel

Gearstick

Chassis

Gearbox

Radiator

Diesel engine (see pages 20-21)

Fuel tank

Turbocharger (see page 23)

Brake

Rear suspension

Leaf suspension

Rear disc brake

Carburetor

Fuel tank

Brake lever

Throttle

Oil cooler

Exhaust

☐ RACING BIKE

Motorcycles have the same systems as cars, but the various parts have to be more compact so that they fit into the bike's smaller frame. They also have to be in a balanced position so that they don't pull the bike to one side.

Rear suspension

Gearbox

Engine

Front suspension

Disc brake

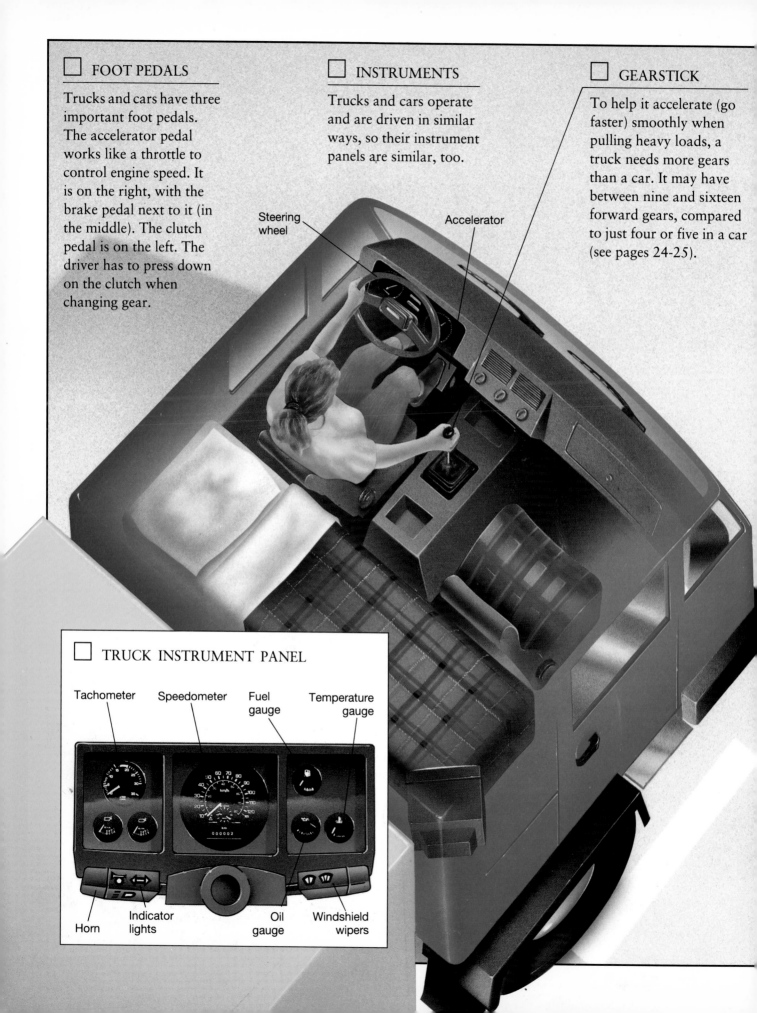

☐ FOOT PEDALS

Trucks and cars have three important foot pedals. The accelerator pedal works like a throttle to control engine speed. It is on the right, with the brake pedal next to it (in the middle). The clutch pedal is on the left. The driver has to press down on the clutch when changing gear.

☐ INSTRUMENTS

Trucks and cars operate and are driven in similar ways, so their instrument panels are similar, too.

☐ GEARSTICK

To help it accelerate (go faster) smoothly when pulling heavy loads, a truck needs more gears than a car. It may have between nine and sixteen forward gears, compared to just four or five in a car (see pages 24-25).

Steering wheel

Accelerator

☐ TRUCK INSTRUMENT PANEL

Tachometer   Speedometer   Fuel gauge   Temperature gauge

Horn   Indicator lights   Oil gauge   Windshield wipers

AT THE CONTROLS

The driver of a motorcycle, car, or truck is surrounded by controls and instruments that allow the vehicle to be driven safely. Instruments are important because they monitor the vehicle systems, telling the driver whether things are operating smoothly and warning when things go wrong.

A fault in one system may cause serious problems in another. The engine can be badly damaged if the cooling system fails, for example, or if the oil leaks out. Keeping an eye on instruments such as the temperature and oil gauges allows the driver to spot problems and deal with them quickly.

The main instruments for measuring speed are the speedometer and the tachometer. The speedometer shows the speed at which the vehicle is traveling along the ground in mph. The tachometer (or rev. counter) shows how fast the engine is running in revolutions per minute (rpm). The odometer records the distance traveled.

☐ GEAR LEVER

The gear lever is operated by the rider's left foot. Different gears are selected by pressing down or raising the lever.

☐ THROTTLE

The rider controls the bike's speed with a throttle handgrip. Twisting the throttle increases or decreases the fuel-air flow into the engine, speeding it up or slowing it down.

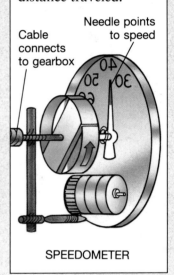

Cable connects to gearbox

Needle points to speed

SPEEDOMETER

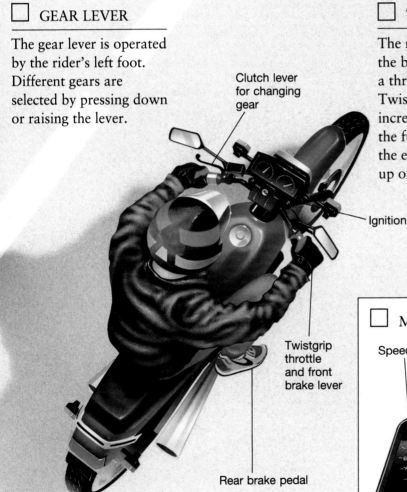

Clutch lever for changing gear

Ignition

Twistgrip throttle and front brake lever

Rear brake pedal

☐ MOTORCYCLE INSTRUMENT PANEL

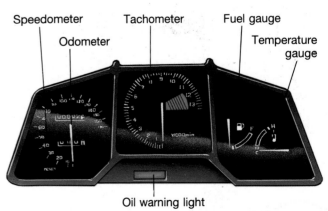

Speedometer

Odometer

Tachometer

Fuel gauge

Temperature gauge

Oil warning light

THE SUSPENSION

Energy cannot be created or destroyed. It can only be changed from one form to another. The kinetic (movement) energy used to squash a spring isn't lost. It is stored by the spring, and let go as kinetic energy again when the spring bounces back.

Travel would be very uncomfortable without the suspension system. This is made up of springs and shock absorbers which swallow up knocks and jolts, letting the wheels follow the ups and downs of bumpy roads, while the rest of the vehicle moves along more smoothly above them.

All land machines need a good suspension system to stop the driver and passengers bouncing around. Off-road vehicles like the one shown here need an especially rugged system to allow them to cope with rough ground.

☐ TIRES — RIDING ON AIR

Tires are made from rubber and filled with air. Rubber is a flexible (stretchy) material, and it can swallow up small bumps. When a tire is squashed by a bump, the air inside also helps, by spreading the shock around the whole tire.

☐ SPRINGS AND SHOCK ABSORBERS

Shock absorbers stop springs bouncing back too quickly. After a spring is compressed (squashed) by a vehicle going over a bump, it tries to bounce back. It is slowed by the thick oil that the piston moves through. Holes and valves in the piston head allow it to move up the cylinder more quickly, to absorb shocks, than back down again.

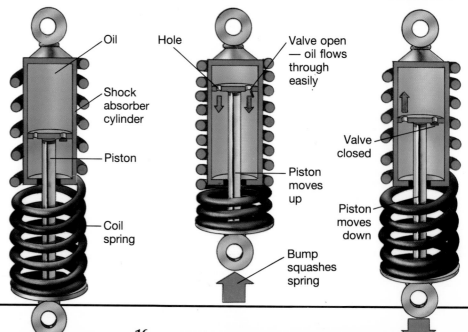

Oil

Shock absorber cylinder

Piston

Coil spring

Hole

Valve open — oil flows through easily

Piston moves up

Bump squashes spring

Valve closed

Piston moves down

☐ SOFT SEATING

Off-road vehicles have springier seats than normal cars, to help them to absorb bumps.

☐ INSIDE OUT

This off-road buggy's suspension system is easy to see because the huge coil springs are outside the body. In most road vehicles, the suspension is hidden inside (see page 27).

☐ LEAF SPRINGS

Leaf springs are made from strips of metal, not coils. When the wheel bounces up, the strips bend to absorb the shock.

Leaf spring   Damper

☐ AIR SUSPENSION

Some trucks are fitted with air-filled rubber bags called bellows, instead of metal springs, to help support their heavy loads.

Air

TEST IT OUT!

Place a ruler half on a table (weighted down by a heavy book) and half off. Then bend the free end of the ruler down a little and put a coin on it. The energy you use to bend the ruler will be stored inside it, like the energy in a spring. When you let the ruler go, the energy will instantly be released as kinetic energy (movement) and sound. The end of the ruler will bounce up, sending the coin flying into the air.

ENGINE POWER

Combustion, or burning, is a chemical reaction between fuel and the oxygen in air. It cannot take place without oxygen. You can prove this if you light two candles, then cover one with a jar.

Things cannot burn without oxygen

The covered candle will go out as soon as it has used up the oxgyen trapped under the jar.

Combustion sets free the energy that is stored or locked up in the fuel. The released energy takes many forms, including heat, light, sound, and kinetic energy.

The most important vehicle system of all is the engine, because this is where the power to move comes from.

Most road vehicles are driven by gasoline engines. In these engines, the chemical energy stored in gasoline is set free and changed into kinetic (movement) energy to drive the vehicle's wheels. Because the energy is released inside the engine, by combustion (burning), these engines are also known as internal combustion engines.

☐ INSIDE ENGINES

Combustion takes place in cylinders inside the engine. One cylinder is shown opposite, in cross-section. Most engines have between two and eight cylinders.

1 MIXING

The correct amounts of fuel and air for burning are mixed in the carburetor. Air flowing in sucks up a needle fixed to a piston, unblocking the fuel pipe and allowing in fuel.

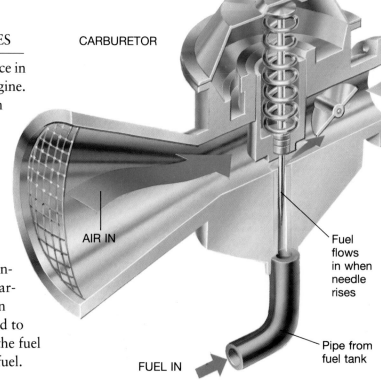

CARBURETOR

AIR IN

Fuel flows in when needle rises

Pipe from fuel tank

FUEL IN

☐ FOUR-STROKE ENGINE CYCLE (most cars, trucks, buses, and other large vehicles)

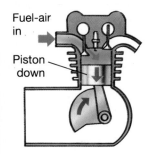

Fuel-air in

Piston down

1. Induction: fuel-air mixture is sucked in.

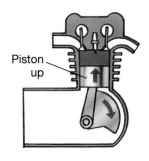

Piston up

2. Compression: piston squashes fuel-air mixture.

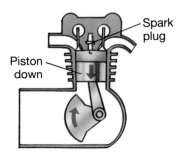

Spark plug

Piston down

3. Ignition and power: fuel-air mixture is ignited by spark.

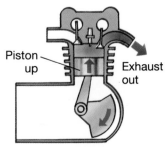

Piston up

Exhaust out

4. Exhaust: piston forces out waste gases.

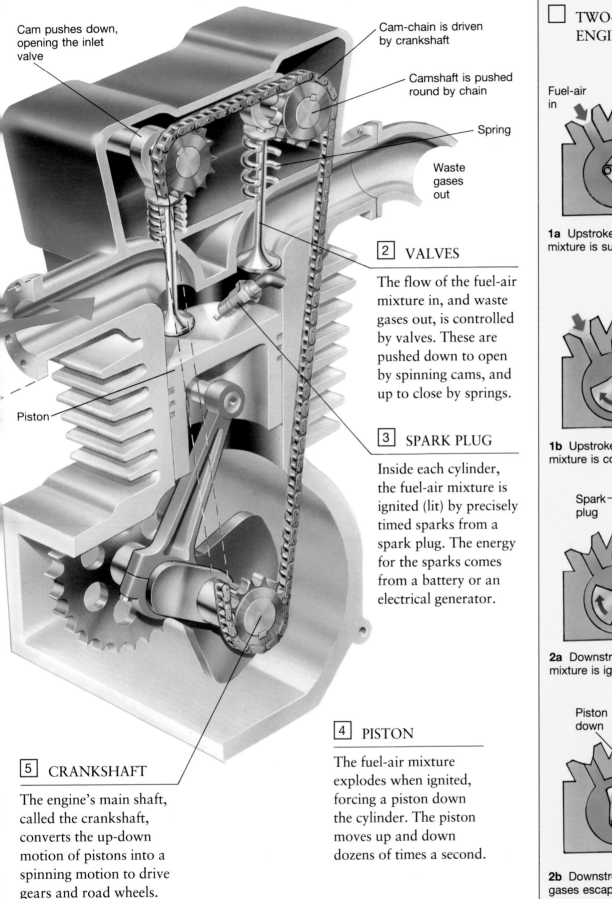

Cam pushes down, opening the inlet valve

Cam-chain is driven by crankshaft

Camshaft is pushed round by chain

Spring

Waste gases out

Piston

2 VALVES

The flow of the fuel-air mixture in, and waste gases out, is controlled by valves. These are pushed down to open by spinning cams, and up to close by springs.

3 SPARK PLUG

Inside each cylinder, the fuel-air mixture is ignited (lit) by precisely timed sparks from a spark plug. The energy for the sparks comes from a battery or an electrical generator.

4 PISTON

The fuel-air mixture explodes when ignited, forcing a piston down the cylinder. The piston moves up and down dozens of times a second.

5 CRANKSHAFT

The engine's main shaft, called the crankshaft, converts the up-down motion of pistons into a spinning motion to drive gears and road wheels.

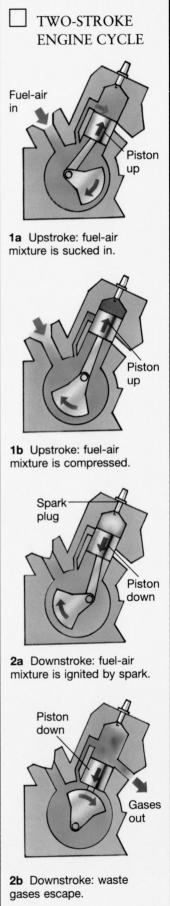

☐ TWO-STROKE ENGINE CYCLE

Fuel-air in

Piston up

1a Upstroke: fuel-air mixture is sucked in.

Piston up

1b Upstroke: fuel-air mixture is compressed.

Spark plug

Piston down

2a Downstroke: fuel-air mixture is ignited by spark.

Piston down

Gases out

2b Downstroke: waste gases escape.

Gases are made of tiny molecules that are always moving. If a gas is compressed into a smaller space, the work done in squashing it turns into heat. This raises the temperature of the gas.

If you compress air in a bicycle pump, by pumping with a finger blocking the end, you'll feel it heat up. In a diesel engine, compression makes air so hot it ignites diesel oil.

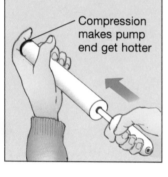

Compression makes pump end get hotter

DIESEL ENGINES

Most trucks, and some cars, are powered by internal combustion engines called diesel engines, after their German inventor Rudolf Diesel (1858-1913).

Diesel engines work differently from gasoline engines. They use diesel oil, which is thicker than gasoline and can be ignited in a different way. In gasoline engines the fuel-air mixture is lit by electric sparks. In diesel engines, air is compressed, or squeezed, until it gets so hot that it ignites the fuel.

☐ DIESEL ENGINE

The main parts of a diesel engine look much like those of a gasoline engine, and they do the same job. But a diesel engine must be made stronger to withstand the greater pressures of the air compression (squeezing) that takes place inside it.

☐ FUEL TANK

In trucks, diesel oil is stored in a large tank behind the cab. From here, it is pumped through pipes to the engine.

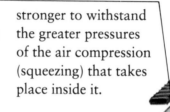

TEST IT OUT!

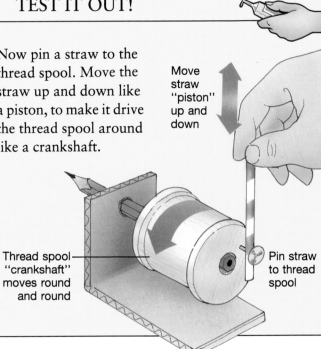

In gasoline and diesel engines, up-down motion has to be changed into rotary motion to turn wheels. This is done by the way the piston and crank-shaft move together.

You can see how they work if you make an L-shaped cardboard bracket. Push a pencil through the upright end and slide a thread spool over the pencil.

Now pin a straw to the thread spool. Move the straw up and down like a piston, to make it drive the thread spool around like a crankshaft.

Move straw "piston" up and down

Thread spool "crankshaft" moves round and round

Pin straw to thread spool

BATTERY

A diesel engine has no spark plugs, but diesel vehicles still need a battery to supply electric current to the lights, instruments, and engine starter motor.

DIESEL CARS

Although diesel engines use less fuel than gasoline engines, and are therefore cheaper to run, it is not yet common for cars to be fitted with them. Diesel engines can be just as powerful as gasoline engines.

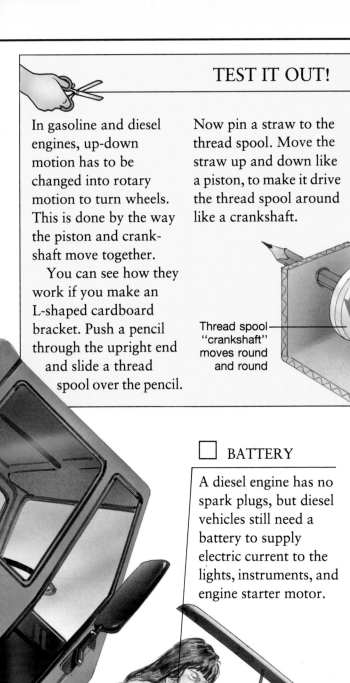

DIESEL ENGINE CYCLE

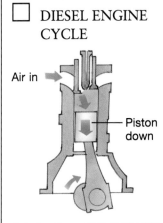

Air in

Piston down

1 Induction: air is sucked in.

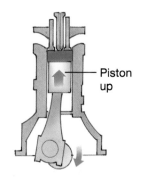

Piston up

2 Compression: piston squashes air to heat it.

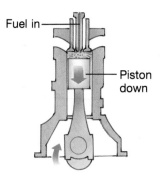

Fuel in

Piston down

3 Ignition and power: fuel is injected and ignites.

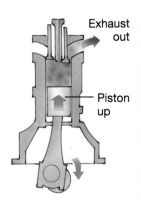

Exhaust out

Piston up

4 Exhaust: piston forces out waste gases.

Power is the rate at which energy is changed from one form into another. It is measured in watts. A 100-watt light bulb, for example, changes electric current into light twice as quickly as a 50-watt bulb does.

The power of early engines was measured in horsepower (hp). One hp was equal to a horse lifting a 100-pound weight at a speed of 330 feet per minute. Modern car engines are measured in brake horsepower (bhp), and 1 bhp equals 745.7 watts.

ROTARY ENGINES

The one big disadvantage of both gasoline and diesel engines is that power is wasted converting the up-down motion of pistons into rotary motion to turn the wheels. An engine with rotating pistons ought to be a lot simpler and more powerful. The Wankel engine, built by Felix Wankel in 1957, was the first engine in which this idea was put into practice.

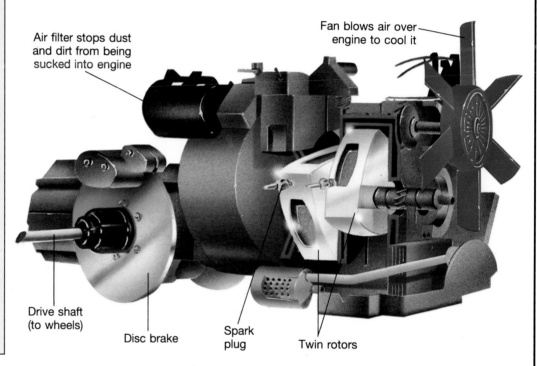

Air filter stops dust and dirt from being sucked into engine

Fan blows air over engine to cool it

Drive shaft (to wheels)

Disc brake

Spark plug

Twin rotors

☐ ROTARY ENGINE CYCLE

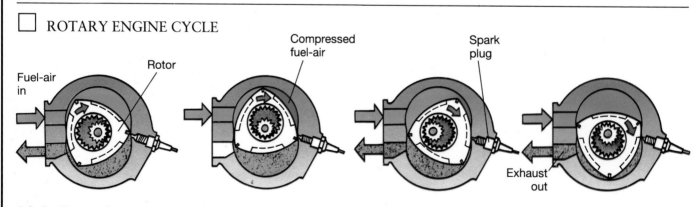

Fuel-air in

Rotor

Compressed fuel-air

Spark plug

Exhaust out

1 Induction: turning rotor sucks in mixture of fuel (gasoline) and air.

2 Compression: fuel-air mixture is squashed as rotor carries it around.

3 Ignition and power: compressed fuel-air mixture is ignited by spark.

4 Exhaust: explosion makes rotor continue to turn, pushing out the waste gases.

EFFICIENT ENGINES

The power and smooth running of an engine can always be improved. Since power depends on the amount of fuel and air that is burned, some engines are fitted with special pumps called turbochargers which force more air into them.

Fuel also burns more efficiently when it is mixed with the correct amount of air. Many engines have fuel injectors and computers to control this mixture very accurately.

FOCUS ON SAVING FUEL

Gasoline and diesel fuel are made from oil. This is a natural resource (it cannot be manufactured) and one day the Earth will run out of its supply.

To make oil last longer, car makers are building more efficient engines. Using less fuel will also cut the air pollution caused by the exhaust gases that engines give out.

☐ COMPUTER

The computer checks the exhaust gases to make sure all the fuel has burned. If it hasn't, the computer adjusts the fuel-air mixture. This boosts engine power and cuts air pollution.

☐ TURBOCHARGER

This has two fan-like turbines. Engine exhaust gases make one turbine spin, so it drives another one in the air intake. The second turbine forces extra air into the engine.

☐ FUEL INJECTOR

Precise amounts of fuel are sprayed into the cylinder through a fine nozzle. The amount of fuel is controlled by the engine's computer.

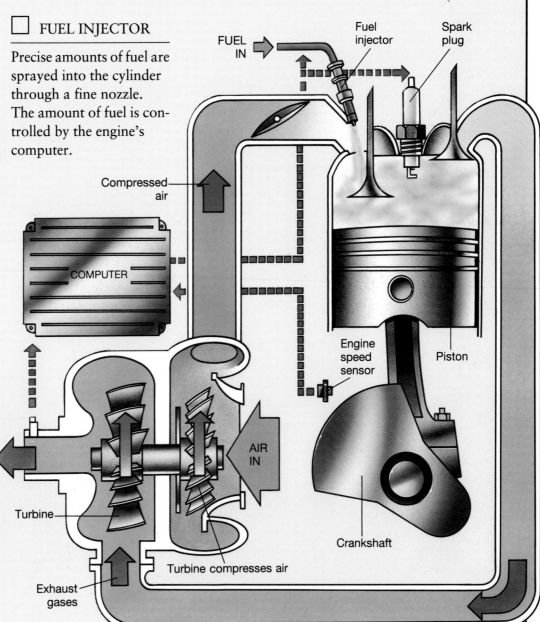

FUEL IN

Fuel injector

Spark plug

Compressed air

COMPUTER

Engine speed sensor

Piston

Exhaust gases

Turbine

AIR IN

Turbine compresses air

Crankshaft

Exhaust gases

FOCUS ON GEARS

Two gears the same size, and with the same number of teeth, will turn at exactly the same speed. Using these gears allows a vehicle's road wheels to turn at the same speed as its engine.

A big gear will turn more slowly than a small one. These gears let a vehicle's road wheels turn more slowly than its engine.

On a bicycle, selecting different gears allows you to pedal slowly and powerfully, even when the wheels are spinning round at top speed.

HIGH SPEED

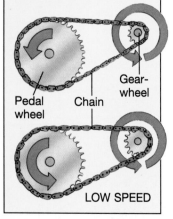

Pedal wheel   Chain   Gear-wheel

LOW SPEED

GEARS — SPEED CONTROL

A vehicle's engine is rarely linked directly to its road wheels. If it were, the vehicle wouldn't be able to travel at much less than 45 mph (75 km/h), since this is the minimum speed at which an engine can run without stalling.

Power is therefore sent from the engine to the road wheels through a system of toothed wheels called gears. Because of the special way gears work, they allow the road wheels to turn at a different speed from the engine. The whole system is called the transmission ("transmit" means send), and its main parts are the clutch, the gearbox, and the final drive (see page 26).

(see page 26).

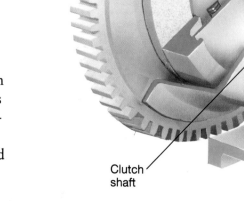

1 CLUTCH

The basic clutch is made up of two plates, one fixed to the engine crankshaft and the other to the clutch shaft.

The plates are usually held against each other by springs so that they spin together. When the driver presses down on the clutch pedal, the plates separate. This breaks the connection between the crankshaft and the clutch shaft (and therefore between the engine and the road wheels).

Clutch shaft

☐ FAST AND SLOW

A low gear enables the engine, running at high speed, to turn the wheels slowly. In a high gear, the wheels turn as fast as the engine crankshaft.

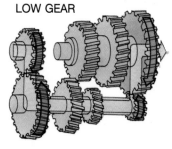

LOW GEAR

Slow spin

Fast spin

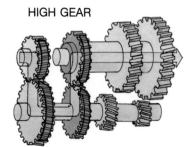

HIGH GEAR

Fast spin

Fast spin

2 CHANGING GEAR

When the clutch pedal is pressed down, the driver can use the gear lever to select a new gear. Gear positions are usually printed on the gear lever. The gearbox shown here has five forward gears and one reverse gear.

1st 3rd 5th

Reverse 2nd 4th

3 GEARBOX

Inside the gearbox, sets of differently sized gears allow a number of speeds to be selected.

Gear lever

TEST IT OUT!

Copy the "gears" below on to some stiff cardboard and cut them out. Make two big wheels and one small one. Pin the two big wheels to a board so that their teeth mesh (lock).

Now test them out — a revolution (complete turn) of one wheel will produce a revolution of the other, but in the opposite direction.

Next replace one of the big wheels with the small one. You'll have to turn the small wheel twice to make the big one turn once. In a gearbox, differently sized gears are used in this way to control the power sent from the engine to the road wheels.

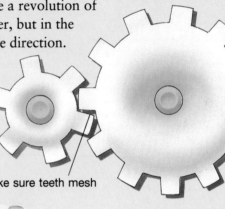

Make sure teeth mesh

4 GEAR SELECTOR

When the driver moves the gear lever, a selector inside the gearbox moves forward or backward, to link different sets of gears together.

Gears spin when a set is locked together

Universal joint allows angle between gearbox and drive shaft to vary, when vehicle bounces over bumps

Drive shaft to differential (see page 26)

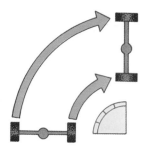

When cornering, the wheels farthest from the curb have to cover more ground, and so spin faster than the inner wheels, to keep up. The arrangement of gears in the differential allows this to happen.

When a vehicle is driving straight, the small differential gears are simply carried around by the crown wheel — they do not spin. They are only "pushed" into action when a vehicle corners. Then their spin lets the two axle shafts and their gears turn at different speeds.

The differential is a special set of gears in the final drive, the part of the transmission system between the gearbox and the road wheels.

The differential does two important jobs. First of all, it reduces the speed of the drive shaft connecting it to the gearbox. Secondly, it allows the road wheels to turn at different speeds when a car or a truck is cornering.

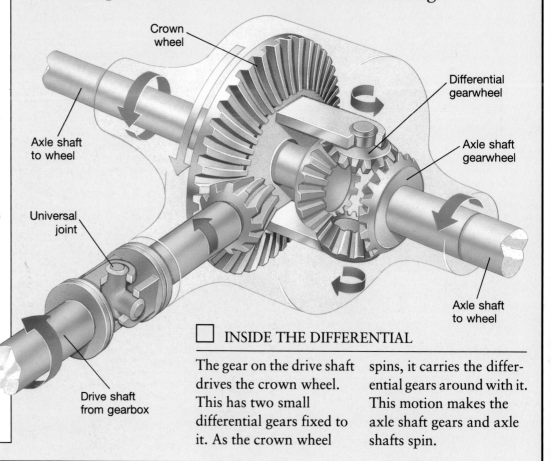

Crown wheel

Differential gearwheel

Axle shaft to wheel

Axle shaft gearwheel

Universal joint

Axle shaft to wheel

Drive shaft from gearbox

☐ INSIDE THE DIFFERENTIAL

The gear on the drive shaft drives the crown wheel. This has two small differential gears fixed to it. As the crown wheel spins, it carries the differential gears around with it. This motion makes the axle shaft gears and axle shafts spin.

☐ DRIVE LAYOUTS

An engine may drive the rear wheels, the front wheels, or all four wheels. Four-wheel drive cars need three differential units — one between each pair of wheels, and a third between front and rear axles.

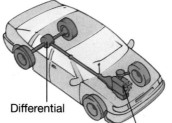

REAR-WHEEL DRIVE

Differential

Engine

FRONT-WHEEL DRIVE

Engine and differential

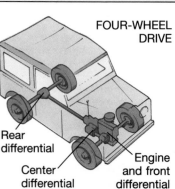

FOUR-WHEEL DRIVE

Rear differential

Center differential

Engine and front differential

STEERING

In most cars and trucks, gears are also an essential part of the steering system. When the driver turns the steering wheel, two gears called the rack and the pinion move against each other. The rack is linked to the wheels and turns them.

The rack-and-pinion gears help the driver by converting a large easy movement of the steering wheel, into a smaller and more powerful movement of the road wheels.

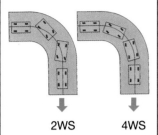

2WS   4WS

Vehicles that use all four of their wheels to steer are now being manufactured. Four-wheel steering allows a vehicle to corner more smoothly and safely. It makes very tight turns possible at low speed, so it also helps when a driver is maneuvering a car to park it in a narrow space.

☐ RACK AND PINION

When the driver turns the steering wheel, a rod turns with it. A pinion gear on the end of the rod also rotates. As it does so, it forces a grooved bar called the rack to one side or the other, pushing the wheels.

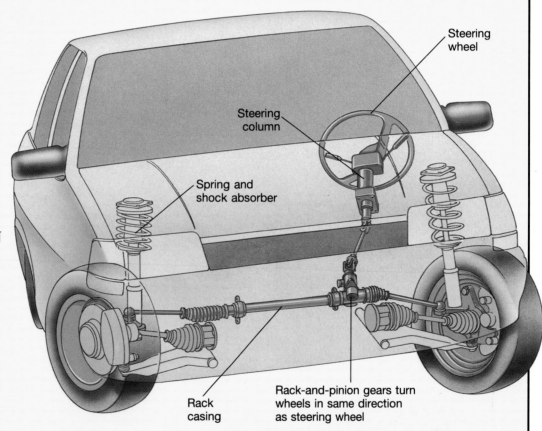

Steering
wheel

Steering
column

Spring and
shock absorber

Rack
casing

Rack-and-pinion gears turn
wheels in same direction
as steering wheel

☐ TYPES OF GEARS

Gears come in different shapes and sizes, but they are always designed so that their teeth mesh (or lock). The more smoothly gears mesh and turn, the less friction there is between them.

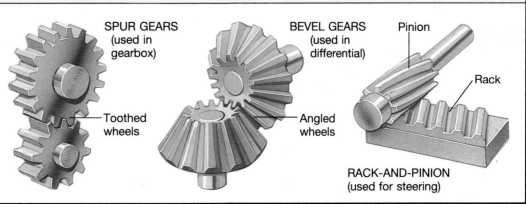

SPUR GEARS
(used in
gearbox)

Toothed
wheels

BEVEL GEARS
(used in
differential)

Angled
wheels

Pinion

Rack

RACK-AND-PINION
(used for steering)

In the past 100 years, land speeds have risen from just 12 mph (20 km/h) to more than 180 mph (300 km/h)! But vehicles have been made safer. Some cars are now fitted with bags that automatically fill with air in an accident, to cushion the driver and passengers from the impact.

FASTER AND SLEEKER

Vehicles have changed dramatically in shape since the first cars were made in the 1880s. But there is a good reason why the high and boxy vehicles of early years have slimmed down into the sleekly streamlined machines of today.

The ease with which an object pushes through the air around it depends on its shape. At high speeds, the low smooth curves of a streamlined vehicle let it slip through the air far more easily than blunt and boxy hard edges.

☐ BENZ MOTORWAGEN

The first practical gasoline-engine car (below) was a three-wheeler made by Karl Benz of Germany in 1885. It had a top speed of 12 mph (20 km/h).

☐ MODEL T FORD

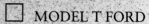

In 1908, less than 25 years after the first car was built, Henry Ford's Model T (above) more than tripled the maximum speed of a car, to 40 mph (64 km/h).

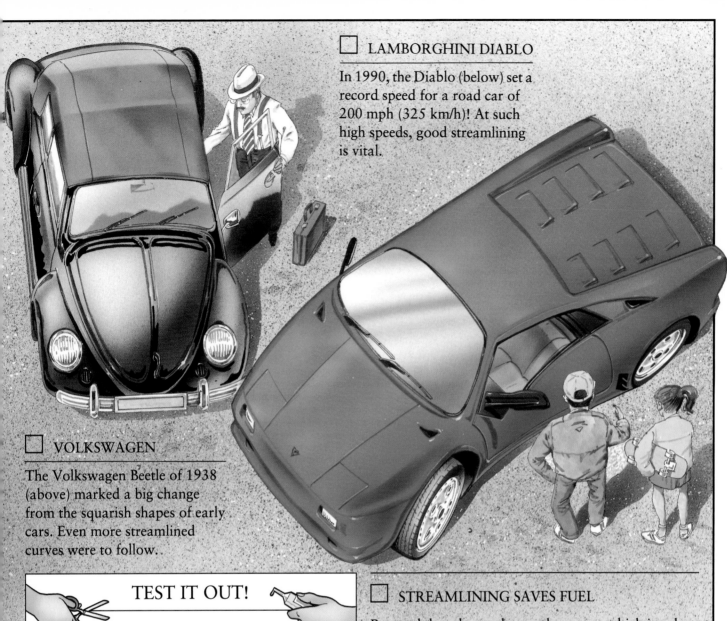

☐ LAMBORGHINI DIABLO

In 1990, the Diablo (below) set a record speed for a road car of 200 mph (325 km/h)! At such high speeds, good streamlining is vital.

☐ VOLKSWAGEN

The Volkswagen Beetle of 1938 (above) marked a big change from the squarish shapes of early cars. Even more streamlined curves were to follow.

TEST IT OUT!

See whether stream-lining works. Let a toy car freewheel down the side of the bath into the water. Mark where it stops with some clay.

Now give the car a blunt cardboard nose and let it run down into the bath again. This time the water will slow the box-shaped car very quickly.

☐ STREAMLINING SAVES FUEL

Research has shown that if a truck is fitted with a more streamlined body, the rate at which it gulps fuel can be reduced by up to 25 percent.

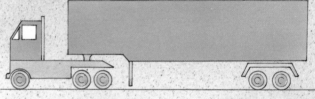

Less streamlined — more air resistance

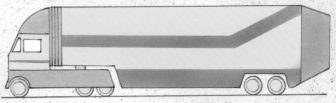

More streamlined — less air resistance

Monorails date back to the 1880s, when the Listowel to Bally-bunion line opened in Ireland. The steam locomotive and train, designed by the French engineer Charles Lartigue, straddled a single A-shaped track.

PEOPLE MOVERS

City transportation systems are designed to move a lot of people quickly from place to place. Machines for "people-moving" include buses and streetcars, as well as electric trains and maglevs. Many of these vehicles are driven by electric motors, which are cleaner than car engines and so help to reduce air pollution. By cutting the number of cars on the road, people movers also help to prevent traffic jams.

☐ MONORAILS

Mono means one, and monorail trains are people movers that run along one rail, not two. The track is usually high above the ground, supported on tall towers called pylons.

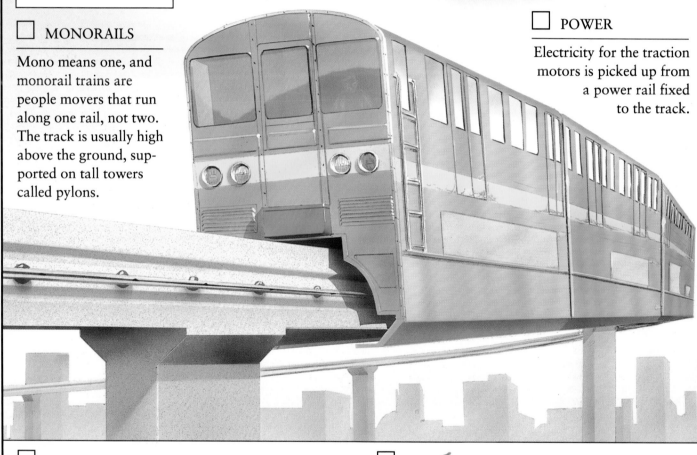

☐ POWER

Electricity for the traction motors is picked up from a power rail fixed to the track.

☐ RIDING ALONG

The running wheels of a monorail are driven by the train's electric traction motors. Guide wheels keep the train on course, and stabilizing wheels stop it from tipping when it is making turns.

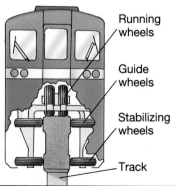

Running wheels

Guide wheels

Stabilizing wheels

Track

☐ ABOVE AND BELOW

There are two types of monorail — straddle and suspension. Straddle trains ride on top of the rail. Suspension trains hang below it. Straddle trains are more popular because they sway less.

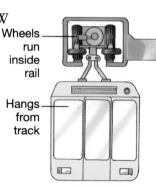

Wheels run inside rail

Hangs from track

A magnet has a North pole and a South pole. Unlike poles (North-South) attract each other. Like poles (North-North or South-South) repel each other.

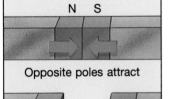

Opposite poles attract

Like poles repel

MAGLEVS

Although they look much like normal monorails, maglev trains are propelled in a completely different way. In place of wheels, a maglev uses powerful magnetic fields to lift itself into the air, and to push itself along a special kind of track. The word "maglev" is short for magnetic levitation (levitation means "rising into the air").

☐ CONTROLS

Some maglevs do not have a driver. Computers make them start and stop at stations.

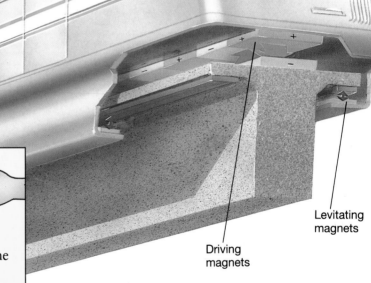

Levitating magnets

Driving magnets

☐ LEVITATION

Magnetic fields are used to hold the maglev just above the track. As the train has no wheels and doesn't touch the track, there is no friction to slow it down.

TEST IT OUT!

You can make and test an electromagnet with a 1.5 volt battery, a nail, and a yard of fine plastic-coated wire.

Wrap the wire tightly around the nail and connect each end to the battery, to switch the magnet on.

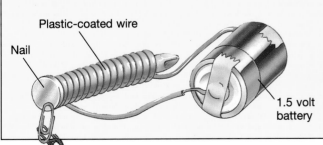

Plastic-coated wire

Nail

1.5 volt battery

☐ PULLING AND PUSHING

Magnets in the track ahead attract the train's magnets, and so pull it forward. The track's magnets are switched to repel the train's magnets as it passes over them, and so push it forward. This is made possible by using electromagnets. In these magnets, the current can be switched to make the poles change North to South, or South to North.

STREETCARS AND TROLLEYBUSES

Streetcars and trolleybuses look rather like buses, but they are powered differently. Instead of gasoline or diesel engines, they have electric traction motors to drive their wheels.

In most cities throughout the world, both these types of transportation were replaced by buses in the late 1950s. Today, electrically powered transportation is making a comeback. New streetcar networks are being built because they can move people more quickly and efficiently than buses or cars, while causing less pollution.

Electric motors convert electrical energy into kinetic (movement) energy. They work because of the forces produced when an electric current flows through a wire near a magnet.

Inside an electric motor, a coil of wire (called the rotor) has magnets or electromagnets around it. When electric current flows through the rotor, the magnets make it move around.

The electric current may come from batteries or be picked up from electric cables.

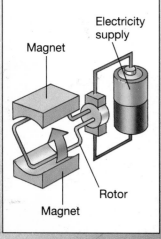

Magnet

Electricity supply

Rotor

Magnet

☐ POWER PICK-UP

Trolleybuses and streetcars pick up electric current to power their traction motors from overhead cables, through a hinged frame called a trolley or a pantograph.

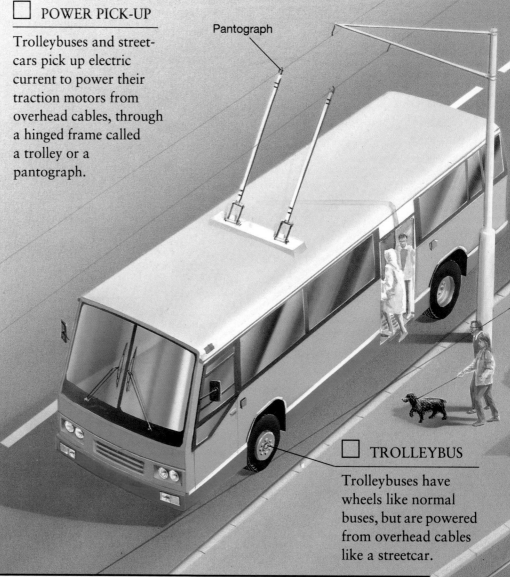

Pantograph

☐ TROLLEYBUS

Trolleybuses have wheels like normal buses, but are powered from overhead cables like a streetcar.

ELECTRIC CARS

It is impractical for electric cars to pick up power from rails or overhead cables, but the batteries available today are large, heavy and inefficient. As a result, electric cars cannot yet go as fast or as far as gasoline-powered cars.

Another disadvantage is that the batteries take several hours to charge, compared to a minute or two to fill a gasoline tank.

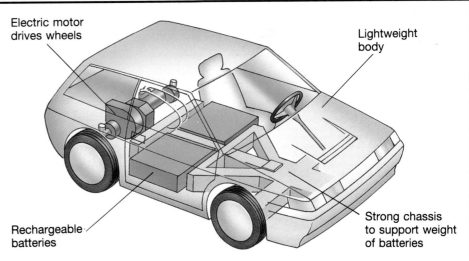

Electric motor drives wheels

Lightweight body

Rechargeable batteries

Strong chassis to support weight of batteries

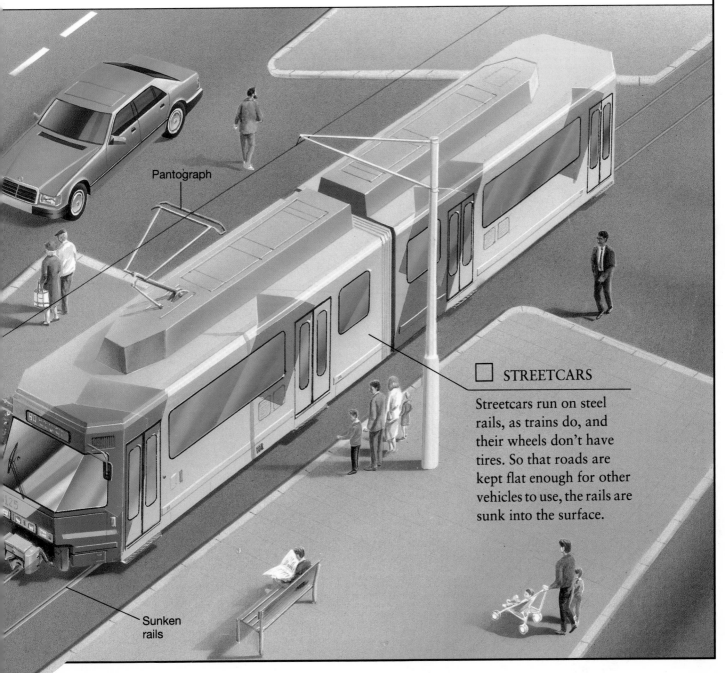

Pantograph

Sunken rails

STREETCARS

Streetcars run on steel rails, as trains do, and their wheels don't have tires. So that roads are kept flat enough for other vehicles to use, the rails are sunk into the surface.

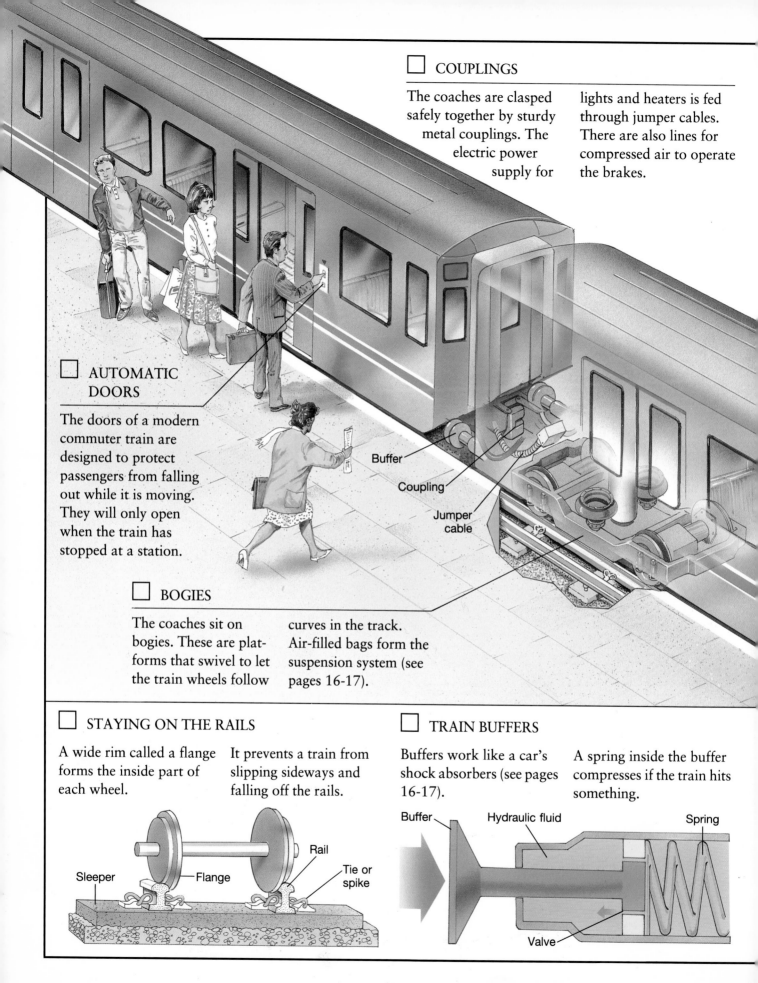

COUPLINGS

The coaches are clasped safely together by sturdy metal couplings. The electric power supply for lights and heaters is fed through jumper cables. There are also lines for compressed air to operate the brakes.

AUTOMATIC DOORS

The doors of a modern commuter train are designed to protect passengers from falling out while it is moving. They will only open when the train has stopped at a station.

Buffer

Coupling

Jumper cable

BOGIES

The coaches sit on bogies. These are platforms that swivel to let the train wheels follow curves in the track. Air-filled bags form the suspension system (see pages 16-17).

STAYING ON THE RAILS

A wide rim called a flange forms the inside part of each wheel. It prevents a train from slipping sideways and falling off the rails.

Rail

Sleeper — Flange

Tie or spike

TRAIN BUFFERS

Buffers work like a car's shock absorbers (see pages 16-17). A spring inside the buffer compresses if the train hits something.

Buffer   Hydraulic fluid   Spring

Valve

RUNNING ON RAILS

The ideal vehicle has just enough friction between its wheels and the ground to make it move, but as little friction as possible elsewhere once it is moving. A vehicle with smooth steel wheels, rolling on smooth steel rails, is very efficient. There is so little friction between the wheels and the rails that a railroad locomotive can pull a much heavier load than a road vehicle with an equally powerful engine.

Trains are driven either by electric motors or by diesel engines. Electric trains pick up current from a third rail laid on the ground, or from an overhead cable called a catenary.

FOCUS ON COMPUTERS

The city of San Francisco is served by an automatic railroad system called BART (Bay Area Rapid Transit).

BART trains are completely controlled by computers. These are programmed to run everything, from the trains' speed, to the opening and closing of doors.

☐ MOTORS

This train is propelled by electric traction motors fitted inside its bogies. There are two motors in the traction bogie, one for each set of wheels. The motors draw power from an electrified third rail.

Gears between the motor and the wheels work like the gears of a car (see pages 24-25) to let the wheels turn more slowly than the engine.

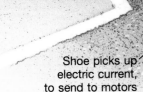

Electrified third rail

Shoe picks up electric current, to send to motors

Traction motor

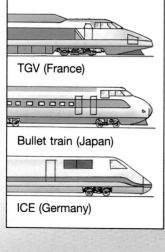

TGV (France)

Bullet train (Japan)

ICE (Germany)

HIGH-SPEED TRAINS

The world's fastest passenger trains operate on long routes between cities. To cut air resistance and help them to achieve average speeds of 90 to 150 mph (150 to 250 km/h), they all have rounded sloping noses and sleek streamlined shapes.

All of these high-speed trains are electrically powered. Some take electric current from overhead wires to power the traction motors that drive their wheels. Others, called diesel-electrics, use a diesel engine to generate the electricity they need. Diesel-only locomotives are only used to pull freight trains, because they cannot accelerate quickly.

☐ DRIVING THE TRAIN

The driver of a high-speed train sits in front of an instrument panel which is similar to that of a car.

The instruments give the driver important information about the train's speed and systems.

Engineer's instrument panel

Headlights

Batteries can provide back-up power

High-speed trains have large onboard traction motors

Front bogie

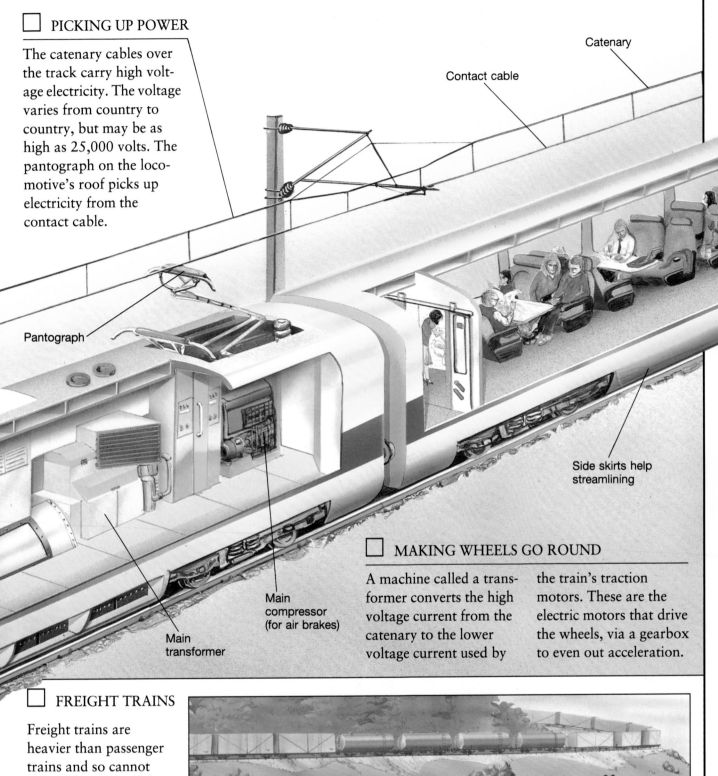

☐ PICKING UP POWER

The catenary cables over the track carry high voltage electricity. The voltage varies from country to country, but may be as high as 25,000 volts. The pantograph on the locomotive's roof picks up electricity from the contact cable.

Catenary

Contact cable

Pantograph

Side skirts help streamlining

Main compressor (for air brakes)

Main transformer

☐ MAKING WHEELS GO ROUND

A machine called a transformer converts the high voltage current from the catenary to the lower voltage current used by the train's traction motors. These are the electric motors that drive the wheels, via a gearbox to even out acceleration.

☐ FREIGHT TRAINS

Freight trains are heavier than passenger trains and so cannot travel as fast. In some countries, several diesel locomotives work together to haul heavy freight trains that may be over 2½ miles (4 km) long!

MAKING TRACKS

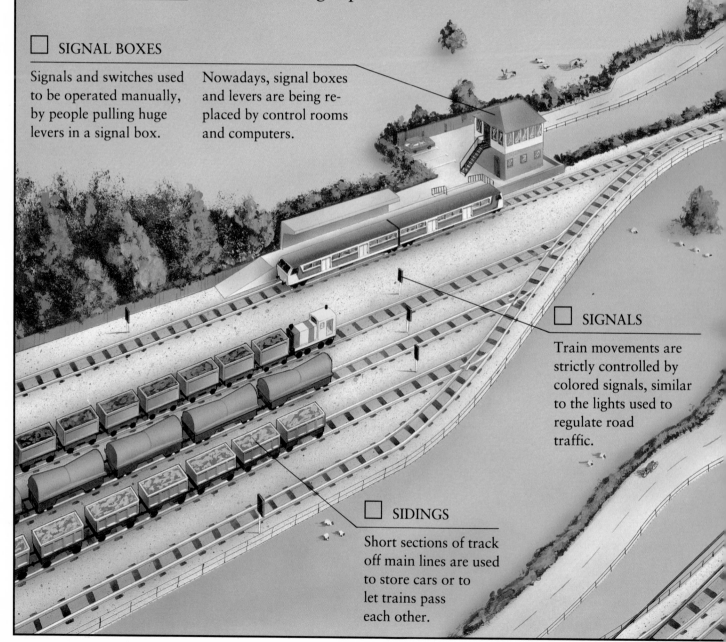

<table>
</table>

FOCUS ON FRICTION

Trains cannot climb slopes easily because there is little friction between wheels and rail, so they can't grip enough. Tracks are kept level by cutting them through hills or building them up on embankments.

The country with the world's biggest railroad network is the United States. If all of its track was laid end to end, it would stretch around the equator more than seven times, or reach three-fourths of the way to the Moon!

In Britain, 15,000 passenger trains run every weekday. It takes a good deal of planning and organization to ensure that trains throughout the whole country run safely and arrive in the right place at the correct time.

☐ SIGNAL BOXES

Signals and switches used to be operated manually, by people pulling huge levers in a signal box.

Nowadays, signal boxes and levers are being re-placed by control rooms and computers.

☐ SIGNALS

Train movements are strictly controlled by colored signals, similar to the lights used to regulate road traffic.

☐ SIDINGS

Short sections of track off main lines are used to store cars or to let trains pass each other.

SWITCHES

Trains can't be steered like road vehicles. They need movable sections of track called switches, to allow them to switch from one line to another.

GRADE CROSSING

When a train approaches a grade crossing, an alarm sounds and lights flash to warn drivers on the road to stop. Then barriers are lowered across the road. Some crossings are automatic, others are operated from a control room.

SWITCHING

Switches are movable sections of track that allow lines to divide.

The new track layout sends the train in a different direction.

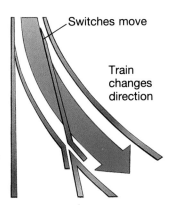

Train travels straight ahead

Switches move

Train changes direction

WATCHING SIGNALS

The colored signal lights by the side of the track are operated electronically, from signal boxes or control rooms.

A green light shows the engineer that the line ahead is clear and it is safe to continue.

Yellow lights warn the engineer to slow down, ready to stop at a red light ahead.

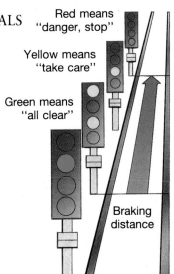

Red means "danger, stop"

Yellow means "take care"

Green means "all clear"

Braking distance

IN THE CONTROL ROOM

In a modern control room, signal operators watch electronic "maps" of the railroad lines. Trains show up as sets of red lights moving along a map. Each train is identified by a number, which moves with it from map to map.

Signal no. 46	Train number	Signal no. 47	Train number
T30	Track 31	T32	Track 33

Red lights show where train IS11 is as it moves from one section of track to another

INDEX

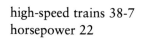

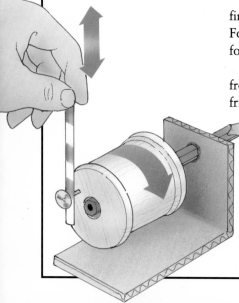